Esther

30 Daily Insights from God's Word by **Peter Lau**

Discovery House is affiliated
with Our Daily Bread Ministries.

Requests for permission to quote
from this book should be directed to:
Permissions Department
Discovery House
P.O. Box 3566
Grand Rapids, MI 49501
Or contact us by email at
permissionsdept@dhp.org

Design by Joshua Tan
Typeset by Grace Goh

ISBN 978-1-913135-10-2

Printed in the United Kingdom
Second Printing in 2020

Foreword

For some of us, our first experience of the book of Esther was in Sunday School. A simplified version of the story presents Esther as winning a beauty pageant. A Jewish orphan from unfortunate circumstances, she rises to become the Queen of the Persian Empire. She then lives happily ever after. A Jewish Cinderella, if you like.

Yet as we read the narrative more closely, we find some more disturbing elements. For example, God's people are not even described as doing anything religious, like praying. Over the centuries, Christian readers have also found it hard to understand the book. How do we evaluate the actions of the Jewish main characters, Mordecai and Esther? What are we to make of all the killing at the end of the book? What has a Jewish festival that celebrates this event—Purim—got to do with Christians today?

Underlying these issues is a more pressing question: where is God? He is not named even once in the entire story.

What we will find as we read and reflect on the book of Esther is that God is not absent, but hidden. And as the "coincidences" in the book pile up, we are left with the conclusion that it must be God's hidden hand behind the series of dramatic reversals that lead to His people's deliverance.

May God grant us fresh insights from His Word in the book of Esther. Insights into His ways as we live outside our Promised Land, in a world where He often seems absent. Insights into how we can live wisely as His people, in a world that is often hostile. And perhaps most of all, a fresh appreciation of His faithfulness to us in Jesus, in whom we've received the greatest deliverance.

To God be the glory,
Peter Lau

We're glad you've decided to join us on a journey into a deeper relationship with Jesus Christ!

For over 50 years, we have been known for our daily Bible reading notes, *Our Daily Bread*. Many readers enjoy the pithy, inspiring, and relevant articles that point them to God and the wisdom and promises of His unchanging Word.

Building on the foundation of *Our Daily Bread*, we have developed this devotional series to help believers spend time with God in His Word, book by book. We trust this daily meditation on God's Word will draw you into a closer relationship with Him through our Lord and Saviour, Jesus Christ.

How to use this resource

READ: This book is designed to be read alongside God's Word as you journey with Him. It offers explanatory notes to help you understand the Scriptures in fresh ways.

REFLECT: The questions are designed to help you respond to God and His Word, letting Him change you from the inside out.

RECORD: The space provided allows you to keep a diary of your journey as you record your thoughts and jot down your responses.

An Overview

The book of Esther is set in the period after the Babylonian exile, in the capital city Susa during the reign of the Persian Empire. It was the great world empire after the Babylonian Empire (539 BC), until it fell to the Greek Empire under Alexander the Great (333 BC). The king in the Esther narrative is Xerxes (also known as Ahasuerus; Esther 1:1), who reigned from 486–465 BC. He succeeded his father Darius I (reigned 522–486 BC), during whose reign the rebuilding of the Jerusalem Temple was completed (Haggai 2:1–9; Ezra 6:15; 516 BC). His predecessors were Cambyses II (530–522 BC) and Cyrus (559–530 BC), under whom the exiles were allowed to return and rebuild Jerusalem and the temple (539 BC; 2 Chronicles 36:22–23; Ezra 1:1–4). Most Jews remained in the diaspora, however, including the Jewish main characters in the Esther narrative, Mordecai and Esther. The ancestors of these cousins had been deported when Babylonian King Nebuchadnezzar destroyed Jerusalem (2 Kings 25:1–21; Esther 2:5–6).

The plot of the book of Esther can be structured as a story of reversals. From the time of Haman's promotion (D) and edict to destroy the Jews (E), everything goes downhill. The turning point is a seemingly unremarkable event—the king can't sleep, which eventually leads to a royal procession honouring Mordecai (H). This in turn triggers a series of "coincidental" events, which lead to God's deliverance of the Jews and the destruction of their enemies.

The Structure of Esther

A: Greatness of Xerxes (1:1–8)

A': Greatness of Xerxes and Mordecai (10:1–3)

B: Banquets of the Persians (1:1–8)

B': Banquets of the Jews (9:20–32)

C: Esther identifies as a Gentile (2:10–20)

C': Gentiles identify as Jews (8:17)

D: Elevation of Haman (3:1)

D': Elevation of Mordecai (8:15)

E: Haman's edict to destroy the Jews (3:12–15)

E': Mordecai's edict to save the Jews (8:9–14)

F: Mordecai–Esther exchange (4:10–16)

F': Xerxes–Esther Exchange (7:1–6)

G: Esther's first banquet (5:6–8)

G': Esther's second banquet (7:1–6)

H: Royal Procession (6:1–14)

Key Verse

"For if you remain silent at this time, relief and deliverance for the Jews will arise from another place, but you and your father's family will perish. And who knows but that you have come to your royal position for such a time as this?"
—Esther 4:14

[1] Slightly adapted from Jon D. Levenson, *Esther*, Old Testament Library (Louisville: Westminster John Knox, 1997), 8.

Day 1

Read Esther 1:1–8

As our narrative opens, we are introduced to King Xerxes. He is someone who could probably star in his own reality TV show, "Lifestyles of the Rich and Powerful". As we read in verse 1, he rules over a vast Persian Empire stretching from India to Sudan and spanning three continents—Asia, Africa, and Europe.

The powerful king of Persia loves to display his wealth. In the third year of his reign, he hosts a feast for all his nobles, officials, military leaders, and princes (Esther 1:3). This feast lasts six months! Then he throws another party, this time for the people in the citadel (v. 5). Verse 4 says that "he displayed the vast wealth of his kingdom and the splendour and glory of his majesty." Read verse 6 again and try to visualise the magnificence of the palace and festivities.

Some millionaires walk around in comfortable, worn-out clothes. Others show off their wealth with luxury suits. We know which category King Xerxes falls into. His palace and banquets are extravagant, excessive, and over-the-top.

We see that King Xerxes is no ordinary ruler. Riches and power he possesses in overwhelming abundance, but does he use them well?

When we watch reality TV shows featuring rich and powerful celebrities, we might grow envious. Their opulent lifestyle and widespread influence leave us wishing for just a little of what they have. **But wealth and power are always double-edged; if abused, they will come to define and control our lives.** As the Bible warns: "Do not love the world or anything in the world . . . For everything in the world—the lust of the flesh, the lust of the eyes, and the pride of life—comes not from the Father but from the world. The world and its desires pass away, but whoever does the will of God lives forever" (1 John 2:15–17). And as we'll see in the book of Esther, God remains in control even when foolish or superficial rulers are in power.

ThinkThrough

Read 1 Timothy
6:6–10 and 17–19
to gain a biblical
perspective on
riches and power.
What do you
treasure or rely on?

If you are blessed
with money and
influence, how are
you using them?
What do you love?

Day 2

Read Esther 1:9–15

In Hans Christian Andersen's tale, "The Emperor's New Clothes," a vain ruler parades before his subjects. His clothes are supposedly made from a fabric invisible to the stupid and incompetent, but he is actually wearing nothing at all. Looking past all the pomp and grandeur of his position, what kind of man is King Xerxes?

Just as the king throws banquets, so does the queen. Queen Vashti throws a banquet, only for the women. By the seventh day of the second banquet, King Xerxes is "in high spirits from wine" (Esther 1:10). This is most likely a nice way of saying that he is drunk. Now that his judgement is impaired, we can expect something bad to happen, and it does. He thinks it's a good idea to parade his wife, the queen, in front of a drunken crowd of men. He has shown off his objects of power and wealth, now he wants to show off another object, his wife. He commands his seven eunuchs to summon the queen.

In verse 11, we are twice told about her stunning beauty. In today's language, King Xerxes wants to show off his trophy wife.

But she says, "No."

The king is furious (Esther 1:12). What irony! The most powerful man in the world, who rules over 127 provinces, cannot command the respect of his own wife. The queen won't obey the mighty king.

Humiliated, the king consults his experts in Persian law on what to do next (Esther 1:13).

So far we've looked at one king, King Xerxes. Let's compare him with another king who is also present in this narrative. One is visible while the other is invisible. Although "The kings of the earth rise up and the rulers band together against the LORD and against his anointed", God who rules in heaven scoffs at them (Psalm 2:2–4). The ungodly kings of this world are ultimately powerless against Him. God's anointed king (Acts 4:25–27)— Jesus, the king of the universe, reigns forever. **He is a king of substance who seeks His Father's will and uses His power for righteousness and justice.**

Are there any areas where you thought you were in control but were not? How does knowing that God is in control help you deal with unfairness in life?

How does knowing that God is the ultimate ruler help us deal with unjust rulers in this world?

Day 3

Read Esther 1:16–22

The king's legal advisors have been put in a tight spot. The king has just asked, "According to law, what must be done to Queen Vashti . . . She has not obeyed the command of King Xerxes that the eunuchs have taken to her" (Esther 1:15). Memukan, one of the king's advisors, doesn't answer the question directly. Instead, he sidesteps the issue by giving an alarmist forecast of the consequences of the queen's offence. He speculates that the queen's disobedience will trigger widespread mini-rebellions—wives will now despise and disrespect their husbands throughout the Persian Empire. This will begin immediately in the households of the king's nobles, and will lead to contempt and anger aplenty (vv. 16–18)!

To counter this "dangerous" threat to authority, Memukan then suggests drafting a new Persian law: Queen Vashti is to be barred from entering the presence of the king (Esther 1:19). Ironically, what she refused to do is now a written decree! She is removed as queen and her position will be given to another. The king issues an official royal edict that "all the women will respect their husbands" (v. 20)

and that "every man should be ruler over his own household" (v. 22). Any husband who reads this edict must be smirking to himself. I'm picturing all of them strutting around like kings of their own little castles.

And so, the king's decree is dispatched by royal mail to every far-flung corner of his kingdom (Esther 1:22). Ironically, most people in the kingdom would probably not have heard of the king's red-faced moment. But they certainly will now!

As we reflect on the king's edict, we realize how ridiculous it is. You can't legislate for one person to respect another. You can't demand that someone respect you. Sure, we can encourage it, but we know from the apostle Paul that this is only half of the equation in any marriage. **Wives should respect their husbands, yes; but husbands also need to love their wives, "just as Christ loved the church and gave himself up for her" (Ephesians 5:25).** I wonder whether King Xerxes loved his wife Vashti like this.

ThinkThrough

Husbands, do you
love your wives
self-sacrificially like
Christ does? Wives,
do you submit to
your husbands as
the church submits
to Christ?

For those of us who
are not married,
do we submit to
others in the fam-
ily of God out of
reverence for Christ
(Ephesians 5:21)?

Day 4

Read Esther 2:1–11

As the curtain is raised on the next scene, we find King Xerxes sobered up and calmed down. He then remembers that he banished his queen and needs to find a replacement (Esther 2:1). Does he come up with a plan himself? Again, no. The king's "young men" (v. 2 ESV) make a suggestion that we would expect young men to make. They say, "Let a search be made for beautiful young virgins for the king . . . Then let the young woman who pleases the king be queen instead of Vashti" (vv. 2–4). This advice pleases the king.

Then, rather unexpectedly, we are introduced to a Jew, Mordecai (Esther 2:5). As we read on we find out that he has a cousin whom he has brought up as his own daughter. The king is seeking a young, unmarried, beautiful woman. Esther fits the bill and more for she also has a "lovely figure" (v. 7). And she is gathered and taken into the king's harem (v. 8). Here Esther is very successful, pleasing the eunuch in charge of the harem and winning his favour. Soon, she is advanced to the best place in the king's harem (v. 9).

Being a member of the king's harem isn't as glamorous as we might think. Once Esther is in the king's harem, she is essentially a captive, placed in the custody of a eunuch (Esther 2:8).

Historically, the women of a king's harem would be confined to it for life. In a sense, she is a double captive and a victim of circumstances. God's people, including the ancestors of Mordecai and Esther, were also carried away as captives by the Babylonian king Nebuchadnezzar (v. 6; see 2 Kings 25:1–21). Esther had no control over what happened to her ancestors, especially the disobedience that led to their exile in Persia (2 Kings 24:1–4).

But King Cyrus issued a decree allowing the Jews to return to the Promised Land at least fifty years before the time of King Xerxes (2 Chronicles 36:22–23). Esther's ancestors in exile could have returned to their homeland then, but they didn't. If she or her ancestors had returned home, further away from Susa, it might be easier to evade the king's net. Back in the Promised Land she would be less likely to find herself in her current predicament.

God can still use his people outside the Promised Land, like Nehemiah. Although we are not sure why Esther and Mordecai remained in Persia, we do know that God can use flawed, ordinary people to fulfil His purposes. **God can use us wherever we might be.**

ThinkThrough

Do we sometimes think that we are a victim of circumstance or of other peoples' decisions and actions? How can we allow God to use us even in such situations?

Turn to Romans 8:28. How does knowing that God uses every situation for the good of those who love Him provide hope for us?

Day 5

Read Esther 2:12–14

Sometimes the competition to select a new queen for King Xerxes is presented as a beauty pageant. But it's nothing of the sort. No, before a "contestant" even goes to the king, her beauty treatments last a whole year. She is prepared for six months with oil of myrrh and six months with perfumes and cosmetics (Esther 2:12). Then she is allowed to take whatever she wants into the king's bedroom to please him (v. 13). She has one night to satisfy the king in his bed, and then in the morning she returns to be part of his harem, as a concubine, for the rest of her life. Unless of course, she is chosen to be queen. As an orphaned Jewish girl, Esther's chances of being selected out of all the virgins from across the 127 Persian provinces were slim.

So try to put yourself in their position. You're stuck in the king's service; you don't get to go home again; you don't get to marry anyone else. And unless you pleased the king, he won't call you back on another night. The women are treated as objects for the king's pleasure. They are used for his entertainment, then disposed of until he fancies them again—if he ever does (Esther 2:14).

But before you think the king's policy is sexist, observe that the boys don't get away scot-free either. King Xerxes has the power to conscript them too. After some "modification", they become eunuchs in his service, like Hegai and Shaashgaz (Esther 2:8, 14). As eunuchs, they pose less threat to the king and they are less likely to molest his harem of women.

Would you rather be a boy or a girl in the Persian Empire?

Israelite kings were meant to maintain justice, as Solomon prays in Psalm 72:1–2. Yet the prophet Samuel warned that kings would misuse their power (1 Samuel 8:11–18). This became reality in Israelite history, starting with Solomon himself using forced labour in his construction projects (1 Kings 5:13–17).

Nonetheless, not all kings abuse their power for their own pleasure. In the Old Testament, kings such as Hezekiah, Josiah, and especially David were approved by God. These kings anticipate an even better king from David's line. **Christ Jesus did not treat His people as objects. Instead, He loved them so much that He was willing to die for them.** Praise God that we serve such a king!

ThinkThrough

In King David's old age, a search was made for a companion (1 Kings 1:1–3). How was this search different from that of King Xerxes? What does this tell us about King David?

Read Philippians 2:5–11. What did King Jesus willingly give up? How should we respond to Him?

Day 6

Read Esther 2:15–18

We've reached an exciting point in the story: it is Esther's turn to go to the king (Esther 2:15). It is now the seventh year of King Xerxes' reign (v. 16); that is, four years after Queen Vashti has been deposed. In those four years, most historians think that King Xerxes went to wage an unsuccessful war against Greece.

But he's now back, and what is his verdict? Esther wins! (Esther 2:17). To celebrate, King Xerxes proclaims a public holiday and hands out gifts to everyone (v. 18).

Yet as we watch and cheer for Esther's rise from nobody to queen, we might feel a sense of discomfort. Mordecai has forbidden her to make her Jewish identity known (Esther 2:10), and we wonder how much else she might have compromised on. How many of the Old Testament laws did she not keep? Did she break the food laws? Did she rest on the Sabbath? It seems that belonging to God's people must be dangerous in some way. But does she compromise too much to keep her background hidden? After all, she does go along quietly with the contest, and does so well that she ends up marrying a foreign, pagan king.

Then we look at Vashti, who refused to go along with the king. And we wonder if Esther also could have or should have refused to play the game. But it is hard for us to judge her, because who knows what we would have done in her situation?

What we do know is that Esther's situation is true to life. Her dilemma is similar to what many of us experience. We face the difficult task of being in this world but not of this world. We face the temptation of hiding or compromising on our faith to avoid problems. We can compromise on some issues, but when it comes to issues of faith and the gospel we cannot. In the New Testament, James warns us that "friendship with the world means enmity against God" (James 4:4). **As Christians, we must say "no" when we are tempted to compromise our faith and the gospel.**

ThinkThrough

How does Esther's approach to living and working outside the Promised Land compare with those of Daniel and his friends (Daniel 1:1–21)? How can we avoid compromising our faith? What should we look out for?

How might we unknowingly compromise our faith to get ahead or to be accepted by society?

Day 7

Read Esther 2:19–23

In this scene we find more unrest in King Xerxes' kingdom. On the surface there may be banquets and drinking, silver, and sparkling jewels, but there is a darker underbelly. Not everyone living under the king is happy. Two eunuchs have murder on their minds (Esther 2:21).

Our attention, though, is drawn to Mordecai. As Esther's cousin and guardian he had paced around anxiously in the courtyard near the harem to learn what was happening to Esther (Esther 2:11). Now we find him sitting at the king's gate (v. 19), which in those days was where government and business activities were conducted in a city. The Persian gates were large buildings with many rooms where royal officials made legal and administrative decisions. Mordecai was thus probably a low-ranking official in the Persian Empire. Yet his presence at the king's gate allowed him to keep his ear close to the ground.

At the gate, Mordecai hears of an assassination plot by two of the king's eunuchs (Esther 2:22). He manages to foil this conspiracy, saving the king's life, and the eunuchs are impaled on poles as punishment. It is all recorded in the official Persian historical annals, but for some reason, King Xerxes forgets what Mordecai has done (v. 23; 6:2–3). There is, however, another king who won't forget. And as we'll find out later in the story of Esther, God will use this seemingly forgotten footnote of history for greater purposes.

In this scene we find Mordecai going about his usual business, working as an official in the Persian government. He is a member of a minority ethnic and religious group within Persian society. **There is some danger in being a member of God's people. Yet he still seeks to promote the good of the government he works for.** In this way, his actions are consistent with the prophet Jeremiah's advice, to "seek the peace and prosperity of the city to which I have carried you into exile" (Jeremiah 29:7).

We might not always receive immediate recognition for our work. But we must continue to serve in a manner where others can see our good works and give glory to our Father in heaven (Matthew 5:16).

Do you face social
disapproval or even
hostility because of
your faith? In what
ways can you still
serve your society
and seek its
prosperity?

How can we remind
ourselves to keep
working as for the
Lord, even when we
don't seem to get
recognition for our
achievements?

Day 8

Read Esther 3:1–6

Mordecai just foiled an assassination plot, but we don't find Mordecai promoted as we might have expected. Haman is promoted instead (Esther 3:1). All this takes place about five years (v 7) after Mordecai saved the king's life.

Immediately, things grow tense. King Xerxes commands that his servants at the gate bow down and pay homage to Haman. But Mordecai doesn't follow the king's command (Esther 3:2). Why not? The Old Testament law does not forbid Mordecai from bowing. Paying respects to someone doesn't necessarily mean that you are treating them as a god (see Genesis 19:1–3; Numbers 22:31; 1 Kings 1:16; 1 Samuel 24:8). Maybe Mordecai just doesn't like Haman. Or, maybe Mordecai is bitter that Haman was promoted instead of him.

Anyway, the king's servants are as puzzled as we are about Mordecai's refusal to bow. So they keep pestering him over it (Esther 3:3–4). And when Mordecai reveals that he is a Jew, they report it to Haman (v. 4). Haman's enraged response is over the top. Once he learns that Mordecai is a Jew, killing him alone isn't enough. Haman looks for a way to kill all of Mordecai's people (vv. 5–6). He wants to wipe out all the Jews in the Persian Empire.

All this because Mordecai refuses to bow down to him? What an extreme response from Haman! And why did Mordecai refuse to bow in the first place?

A likely reason can be found in their family backgrounds. Haman is described as an Agagite (Esther 3:1). Agag was the Amalekite king who was spared by King Saul. Saul's refusal to obey God by executing King Agag was a major factor that cost Saul his kingship (see 1 Samuel 15). Mordecai is a Jew from the tribe of Benjamin, the same tribe as Saul. One of his ancestors is Kish, Saul's father (Esther 2:5). So, there's bad blood between Haman's ancestors and Mordecai's ancestors. But the enmity goes back even further. In Exodus, when Israel was travelling through the wilderness on the way to the Mount Sinai, the Amalekites came out to fight against Israel (see Exodus 17:8–16). The bitterness is also between Haman's people and Mordecai's people. Indeed, God had commanded that Israel "blot out" the name of Amalek (Deuteronomy 25:19).

We can debate whether Mordecai's action was wise or not. **But if the above reason is true, then he has taken a stand based on principle that leads to him breaking the Persian law.**

Another Jew will bow down to the Persian ruler later in the book of Esther, to plead for the Jews' survival (see Esther 8:3). What light does this shed on Mordecai's refusal to bow?

Peter and the apostles refused to obey human authorities when it clashed with God's commands (see Acts 5:27–29). Can you think of situations where you might need to take a stand based on your Christian principles?

Day 9

Read Esther 3:7–11

As the scene opens we see Haman casting lots (or *pur*). He is superstitious and wants to find the most auspicious date for his scheme (Esther 3:7). With the date set, Haman approaches the king with his request.

Haman uses a mixture of truths, half-truths, and lies (Esther 3:8). It is true that there is a "certain people" (v. 8) dispersed among the peoples in the Persian Empire. It is only half true that "their customs are different" (v. 8) because even though they followed Old Testament laws, Esther must have broken at least some of it in order to live in the king's palace. For instance, she married a foreigner, and she most likely ate defiled food (see Daniel 1). Finally, it is false that "it is not in the king's best interest to tolerate them" (v. 8), because we've just seen that Mordecai saved the king's life.

Then, to put the icing on the cake, Haman throws in a massive bribe of 10,000 talents (around 340 tons) of silver (Esther 3:9). This sum is estimated to be over half of the annual tax revenue of the whole Persian Empire. Maybe Haman thought he would seize this much from the Jews after he wiped them out. In this shrewd way, Haman hoodwinks King Xerxes into agreeing to annihilate God's people.

The deal is then sealed (Esther 3:10). The king hands over his signet ring (a symbol of his authority), along with the money and the Jews for Haman to "do with the people as [he] please[s]" (v. 11). As an avowed "enemy of the Jews" (v. 10), Haman receiving the king's authority to do as he pleases surely spells tragedy for them.

Unfortunately, this hatred against God's people is not just limited to the time of Esther. It has happened all through Israel's history. Even today, there are people out to persecute and kill Christians. At times, our persecutors will use truths, half-truths, and flat-out lies to incite the authorities against us. Jesus describes the devil as "a murderer from the beginning," who uses lies, since "he is a liar and the father of lies" (John 8:44). Slander was used against Jesus to kill Him. Slander was also used against Jesus' followers in Acts 17:6–7.

So, sadly, Haman is not just a one-off. Haman-types have slandered and tried to kill God's people throughout history. They continue to do so today. Yet Jesus assures us that he will be with us by his Spirit, even to the end of the age (John 14:15–17; Matthew 28:20).

How do we see lies being used against Christians today (see John 8:44)? How should we respond?

Read Revelation 2:8–11. The church in Smyrna faced slander and persecution. How have you experienced slander and persecution as a Christian? What encouragement can you draw from Jesus' words?

Day 10

Read Esther 3:12–15

Some Asian parents try to give birth during an auspicious year. Some Asian couples consult the lunar calendar to find an auspicious date to get married. Haman cast lots for the most auspicious month to carry out his scheme (Esther 3:7). It was to "destroy, kill and annihilate all the Jews—young and old, women and children—on a single day" (v. 13). Even as we read it today, the ruthlessness sends a chill down our spines.

The edict is dispatched by royal mail to every corner of the Persian Empire (Esther 3:14). The king and Haman celebrate with wine, but the people are bewildered (v. 15). As Haman and the king sit down to enjoy their drinks, we'll take a step back from the narrative to consider: is there another power at work behind the timing of this terrible edict?

There are two hints that there is.

The decree is written on the thirteenth day of the first month (Esther 3:12). This is a day before Passover (see Exodus 12:1–11). So we wonder: will there be another miraculous deliverance like the Exodus? (We might not notice the significance of the date unless we're Jewish, but it would be like Christmas Eve for them.)

The date that is set for the genocide is the thirteenth day of the twelfth month (Esther 3:13). This is eleven months into the future. Remember that this date was set by Haman casting lots. We recall that Proverbs 16:33 says, "The lot is cast into the lap, but its every decision is from the LORD." And Esther 3:14 says that the decree is proclaimed to "the people of every nationality so that they would be ready for that day". So we wonder: could it be that a hidden hand has set this date so that the Jews also had more time to respond to this decree?

It's not explicitly mentioned if God's hidden hand was behind the choosing of the date. Even so, Haman is still fully responsible for his evil intentions and actions. **In fact, God's plan will be carried out despite the actions of individuals.** This is similar to what happened to Joseph. He was sold into slavery, but rose to a position of authority in a foreign land and rescued his family from famine. His brothers meant to harm him, "but God intended it for good to accomplish what is now being done, the saving of many lives" (Genesis 50:20). Even today, God is intimately and meticulously watching over all of His creation, us included (Matthew 6:26).

ThinkThrough

What comfort can we draw from the truth that God always achieves His purposes?

Read Acts 2:22–23. How did the actions of "wicked men" ultimately lead to our salvation?

Day 11

Read Esther 4:1–11

The next scene shows the effect that the edict has on Mordecai and the Jews. Mordecai tears his clothes, puts on sackcloth and ashes, then wails loudly and bitterly in the middle of the city (Esther 4:1). But something seems to be missing in Mordecai's response. It also seems to be missing in the response of the Jews across the Persian Empire (v. 3): prayer. In fact, outward signs of inward faith are not mentioned in the book of Esther, including prayer. Maybe they were God's people in name only, and didn't pray at all.

But even if that were the case, at least in times of crisis we would expect them to turn to God in prayer. In other books of the Bible, a national crisis usually leads to mourning and fasting, and often triggers repentance and prayer (e.g. Lamentations 3:40–66; Nehemiah 9:1–5). The enormity of the impending disaster probably did prompt Mordecai and the Jews to repent and pray. But it is not mentioned, so the one to whom they turn is hidden.

Mordecai is mourning at the king's gate (Esther 4:2) but Esther is isolated in the harem and needs to be told of his predicament. Upon hearing of it, she is deeply distressed, and tries to soothe him by sending clothes (v. 4). Or, perhaps sending clothes will enable him to access the palace to speak to her directly, since he can't enter the king's gate while wearing sackcloth (v. 2). In any case, he flatly refuses (v. 4). Yet through Hathak, one of the king's eunuchs assigned to attend her, she finds out that Haman has issued a decree to destroy the Jews (vv. 5–9).

Mordecai then commands Esther, "to go into the king's presence to beg for mercy and plead with him for her people" (Esther 4:8). But there's a hitch. Esther can't just approach the king whenever she likes. Just like everyone else, she needs to be summoned. According to Persian law, if she appears before the king unannounced she can be put to death, unless he forgives the intrusion by holding out his golden sceptre (v. 11). And the problem is that Esther hasn't been summoned by the king for thirty days (v. 11).

Remember, the king chose Esther out of all the women in his empire to be his queen. But now it seems his affection for her has gone cold. Esther hesitates because she is not sure whether the king will accept her approach or not.

The tendency to be God's people in name only is found throughout the Bible. God often reminds His people to keep choosing to obey Him (Deuteronomy 30:15–20) and to keep passing on a fresh faith to the next generation (Deuteronomy 6:6–7, 20–25; Joshua 4:21–24). **We must ensure that we have a genuine faith in our Lord Jesus so that we can pass it on.**

ThinkThrough

How would you show your faith to family, friends, and colleagues through the way you live?

How can you have a living, personal relationship with the Lord Jesus? And how can you pass it on to the next generation (2 Timothy 3:14–17)?

Day 12

Read Esther 4:12-17

Esther hesitates but Mordecai isn't so easily put off. Perhaps she's thinking, "I'm the queen and safely tucked away in this palace. Anyway, if I keep my Jewish identity secret I'll be safe from Haman's decree."

Mordecai stops that line of thinking immediately. He says, "Do not think that because you are in the king's house you alone of all the Jews will escape" (Esther 4:13).

"For if you remain silent at this time, relief and deliverance for the Jews will arise from another place, but you and your father's family will perish" (Esther 4:14). Most likely, Mordecai is suggesting that she will be punished for not acting.

In short, Mordecai says, "You think your life is at risk if you go to the king? Your life is at risk if you don't." Faced with that cold hard reality, Esther musters her resolve. She encourages her maids, as well as all the Jews, to fast for her before she approaches the king (Esther 4:16).

So far in the book of Esther, God hasn't been mentioned. He won't be mentioned in the rest of the book either. God's control of events is not specifically stated, which has the effect of placing the spotlight on the roles of the Jews, especially Mordecai and Esther. One effect of hiding God and His actions is that it places more emphasis on us: our action, our initiative, our courage in acting.[2]

Sometimes we need to act with initiative for the sake of God and His people. **God can fulfil His purposes without us. But often He chooses to use us.** It's not that He needs us or else His plans go out the window. And it's not that He only intervenes in the affairs of His world when things go wrong. His hidden hand works even in the everyday events of life.

Often He chooses to use our initiative and our actions to accomplish His ends. But even if we don't act, God will still accomplish His purposes. As Mordecai says to Esther, "if you remain silent at this time, relief and deliverance for the Jews will arise from another place" (Esther 4:14).

[2] See Peter H. W. Lau and Gregory Goswell, *Unceasing Kindness: A Biblical Theology of Ruth*, New Studies in Biblical Theology (Downers Grove: InterVarsity, 2016), 100–101.

What comfort is there in knowing that even if we fail to stand up as Christians, God will still accomplish His purposes?

Are there people we can ask to pray and fast with us as we face suffering for being Christians?

Day 13

Read Esther 4:12–17

Today, we'll focus on the best-known sentence from the book of Esther. Mordecai concludes his argument by asking Esther to reflect on her life: "And who knows but that you have come to your royal position for such a time as this?" (Esther 4:14).

In effect, Mordecai says, "Think about it, Esther: you were an orphaned Jewish girl plucked from obscurity to be queen. Could it be that you have been put in this place of influence for such a time as this? Could a hidden hand be behind your royal position for such a time as this?"

Esther responds by taking the risk of going to the king. As she says, "And if I perish, I perish" (Esther 4:16). She is unsure if she will be successful, yet she courageously decides to act. Although she takes the initiative to act, she knows that she can't control the outcome.

Again, notice that God is hidden. Mordecai could have said, "And who knows but that God has placed you in your royal position for such a time as this?" But he doesn't. Let's think again about why God is hidden in the book of Esther.

It helps if we consider the situation of the Jews in the book of Esther. They are outside the Promised Land. They are a minority people, with a minority religion, living in the Persian Empire. In this situation, it would seem like God is absent or has forsaken them. So the narrative of Esther is written in a way that reflects the reality of God's people outside the Promised Land.

This is similar to the situation of many of us. We, as Christians, are the people of God (see Galatians 3:7, 29). We look forward to our promised inheritance awaiting us in heaven (1 Peter 1:3–5). Some of us might be members of a minority ethnic group in our country. Most of us live in countries where Christianity is a minority religion. Often we feel that God is hidden.

We plod along, day after day, largely without God doing anything spectacular. Many of us won't see a miracle of God. Most of us won't hear God speaking to us directly. **But the book of Esther reveals that even when God seems absent, He is not. He is active in everything, even when His hand is hidden from us.** His hand even works through the ordinary events in our lives, although at times we'll only see it in hindsight.

ThinkThrough

Reflect on your experience of God's actions in your life. Do you see Him at work from day to day? Or, are His "fingerprints" mostly seen when you look back on your life?

How can we respond to the truth that God is always present with us and is always active in our lives?

Day 14

Read Esther 5:1–8

As Esther approaches King Xerxes, we wonder if he will let her in to see him or not. We know her life is at risk. But the king quickly extends his sceptre (Esther 5:1–2). And we let out a sigh of relief. He says to her, "What is it, Queen Esther? What is your request? Even up to half the kingdom, it will be given you" (v. 3). This phrase implies that the king is feeling generous. In the New Testament, King Herod makes the same offer to Herodias' daughter (Mark 6:23).

Talk about King Xerxes giving Esther a blank cheque! I'm sure most of us would have quickly made our request then and there. But Esther doesn't make her request. Instead, she invites the king and Haman to her banquet (Esther 5:4).

They come along to Esther's banquet and the king again asks her to present her request (Esther 5:6). Esther still refuses to make her request (vv. 7–8). We're not told why. Perhaps it wasn't the social custom to make the request so soon. Or perhaps she knows that the way to a man's heart is through his stomach. So the more food and wine, the more likely he'll say yes! Perhaps she sensed it wasn't the right time to ask. Whatever the reason, Esther keeps the king, and us, in suspense.

In approaching the king with her request, Esther seems to be following a careful plan. She dresses up in a way that is befitting a queen (Esther 5:1); she places herself in the right spot to be noticed by the king (vv. 1–2); and she speaks with a submissive tone (vv. 4, 7–8). When she is asked to make her request, her delay also seems to be part of her plan.

Yet plan as she may, we know that in the end, everything that takes place in the world is under God's control. Jesus says that not even a sparrow falls to the ground without God knowing (Matthew 10:29). And as it says in Proverbs 16:9, "In their hearts humans plan their course, but the LORD establishes their steps." Esther follows her plan, but only one person knows if she will be successful.

Clothing often reflects a change in status of the characters in a narrative. Can you see this in the narrative of Esther (compare Esther 4:1–3 with 5:1; 6:7–11; 8:15)?

Consider James 4:13–15. Why can we not make definite plans for our lives? What should be our attitude as we make plans for our life?

Day 15

Read Esther 5:9–14

Haman is over the moon that he's been invited to a special, exclusive meal. It's only the king, the queen, and himself (Esther 5:12). "I'm part of the king's inner circle," he thinks. But his mood soon turns dark when he sees Mordecai at the gate (v. 9).

So he invites his friends over. He starts bragging in front of his friends and his wife. He recounts to them the glory of his riches, his many sons, and how the king has elevated him above the other servants and officials (Esther 5:11). Then he complains that he won't be able to enjoy his intimate meal because Mordecai the Jew remains a thorn in his side (v. 13). Mordecai still refuses to show him honour (v. 9). "Why not do away with him?" suggest his wife and friends. They advise him to build a pole 50 cubits high (22.5 metres, or more than six storeys; an extreme height), and ask the king to impale this pesky Jew on it the next morning (v. 14).

"A perfect solution," thinks Haman, as he orders the pole to be built. Haman can't wait eleven months, when the edict will take effect, to destroy Mordecai; he must be killed now. The exaggerated height of the pole would heighten Mordecai's public shaming. Yet the pole's height is appropriate for Haman also: an oversized pole for his oversized ego.

And that is Haman's major character flaw: he seeks the honour of men. He talks up his possessions and achievements because he wants to be adored for them. They have become his source of honour and pride.

Yet we recall two proverbs:

1. "The LORD detests all the proud of heart. Be sure of this: they will not go unpunished" (Proverbs 16:5).

2. "Pride goes before destruction, a haughty spirit before a fall" (Proverbs 16:18).

There may be a dark cloud on the horizon for Haman.

God's opposition to the proud is repeated in the New Testament (2 Timothy 3:1–5; James 4:6; 1 Peter 5:5). Do you take too much pride in your possessions and achievements?

Read 2 Corinthians 10:17–18. According to Paul, what should we boast in?

Day 16

Read Esther 6:1–6

Our attention now turns to the king. It just so happens that he can't sleep that night. Even after such a happy meal with so much wine! Maybe he's lying awake wondering what his queen will request from him.

Well, what do you do when you can't sleep? I hope you don't play games on your iPad or fiddle with your smartphone, because all the digital excitement will interfere with your sleep patterns. You should read something boring, of course! When people ask if they can read my PhD thesis, I say, "Sure, if you have trouble sleeping!" And when my wife couldn't sleep in the past, she used to pull out the tax guide!

The king orders that the historical chronicles of his reign be brought and read to him (Esther 6:1). Maybe he hopes the boring recitation will help him sleep. The king's readers just so happen to choose a particular volume. This volume just so happens to fall open at the page that describes how Mordecai saved the king's life (as we read in Esther 2:21–23).

"What honour and recognition has Mordecai received for this?" asks the king (Esther 6:3). "Nothing," reply the king's attendants (v. 3).

The king realises that not honouring Mordecai is a serious oversight that he needs to correct. At that moment, it just so happens that Haman steps into the king's court. He can't wait to get Mordecai hanged, so he arrives to work very early. The king asks Haman, "What should be done for the man the king delights to honour?" (Esther 6:6).

It just so happens that the king can't sleep that night. And then it just so happens that he finds out how Mordecai hasn't been rewarded right before Haman can ask about having him hanged. Coincidence?

One way that God's actions are presented in the book of Esther is through these "chance happenings". From our viewpoint, we are surprised that things can just fall into place so easily. But don't be fooled: there are too many "coincidences" in the book of Esther for it to be just luck or chance. Again, it is the hidden hand of God working behind the scenes.

ThinkThrough

Read Acts 17:24–28. How does God guide all people in all places in the world so that we might seek Him?

How has God acted in your life such that you were moved to turn to Him? As you look back at how God saved you, can you identify a chain of events that seem to just fall into place?

Day 17

Read Esther 6:7–11

The king asks Haman, "What should be done for the man the king delights to honour?" (Esther 6:6). Of course, big-ego Haman immediately concludes that the king wants to honour him! "Who is there that the king would rather honour than me?" (v. 6) he thinks.

So what does Haman suggest to the king? "Let them bring a royal robe the king has worn and a horse the king has ridden, one with a royal crest placed on its head" (Esther 6:8). If you recall how Joseph was honoured by Pharaoh (see Genesis 41:42–43), you'll notice that what Haman asks for goes way beyond how Joseph was honoured. Joseph wears a linen garment and gold necklace, rides in the chariot of the second-in-command, and people cry out before him, "Make way!" In comparison, Haman asks for the king's robes (a symbol of his royal power) and horse, and he wants a full phrase of commendation proclaimed by no less than a noble prince (Esther 6:9). Haman already has his signet ring; he might as well ask for the king's wife for the full house! Hold on to that thought; we'll come to it soon enough. Haman could have asked for power or wealth. Instead, what he asks for reveals what he desires the most: honour and adoration.

Part of the irony in this scene is that the king and Haman talk past each other. Thus the king's actual command comes as a huge surprise for Haman. The king says, "Go at once . . . Get the robe and the horse and do just as you have suggested for Mordecai the Jew" (Esther 6:10). What a shock and absolute horror for Haman! The honour is not for him but his archenemy! Even more amusing for us as readers (but more painful for Haman) is how the king's command highlights the very features of Mordecai that eat at Haman. Haman must parade "the Jew" whom he wants to execute around the streets. He must call out about the man who refuses to honour him, "This is what is done for the man the king delights to honour!" (v. 11).

Yet the irony also highlights an ugly effect of pride: it can lead to blindness. **Being so full of ourselves can blind us to what is happening around.** Sure, Haman had some reasons to be proud: receiving the king's signet ring meant that he had been elevated to the equivalent of prime minister, and he had been invited to an exclusive dinner with the king and queen. But if Haman had a sliver of humility, it might have occurred to him to clarify whom the king wanted to honour. Then things might have turned out very differently.

How does Haman's character illustrate this proverb: "When pride comes, then comes disgrace, but with humility comes wisdom" (Proverbs 11:2)?

Read Philippians 2:1–11. How does the example of Jesus spur us to be humble and to look out for the interests of others?

Day 18

Read Esther 6:12–14

After honouring Mordecai, Haman returns to his wife and friends with his tail between his legs (Esther 6:12). He has lost face. He is feeling deeply shamed. When he tells his wife and friends what happened, they respond with something remarkable: "Since Mordecai, before whom your downfall has started, is of Jewish origin, you cannot stand against him—you will surely come to ruin!" (v. 13).

I can just imagine what Haman is thinking: "Oh great, why didn't you tell me that before! You told me to build a pole for him and now you change your tune!"

According to scholars, the word "fall" in the book of Esther is tied to Haman and his fate. He causes the lot to "fall" to determine the day to carry out his edict (Esther 3:7). King Xerxes then tells Haman to carry out all the tasks to honour Mordecai: "Do not neglect anything you have recommended" (6:10), which in Hebrew literally means "do not let a thing fall of all that you have said". Now Haman's advisors tell him that his downfall has begun and certain doom awaits him (v. 13).

Although Haman's advisors only mention "the Jews", the fate of the people of God can't be detached from the actions of God. Thus, God's hidden hand can be detected yet again. His work is even sensed by Gentiles, who anticipate the reversal of the fate of the Jews.

Then, before we know it, Haman is hurried away to Esther's next banquet (Esther 6:14). He will experience more "falling" very soon.

We don't know how these Gentiles can sense Haman's downfall. Perhaps they know something of the history of the Israelites. In the Bible, the survival of God's people bears witness to His power (e.g. Malachi 1:2–5). **Indeed, all God's actions in judgment and salvation testify to all peoples that He is "the Lord" (e.g. Exodus 7:5; Ezekiel 36:23).** Elsewhere in the Bible, foreigners recognise and then respond to who God is. For instance, in the Old Testament there are the sailors on Jonah's boat (Jonah 1:14) and King Nebuchadnezzar (Daniel 3:28–29). In the New Testament, there is the centurion who declares that Jesus is the Son of God (Matthew 27:54). Praise God that He makes His salvation known to all the earth!

ThinkThrough

Read Psalm 98. Who or what "shouts for joy to the LORD" (Psalm 98:4)? From this psalm, name at least two things we can praise God for.

In your life, how can you testify about who God is?

Day 19

Read Esther 7:1–7

We can tell if a person is wise by their actions and their words. As Esther finally makes her request, there are at least three things we can learn from the way she approaches the king.

First, she is *respectful*. She introduces her request with, "If I have found favour with you, Your Majesty, and if it pleases you" (Esther 7:3). If we compare Haman's speech to the king in the previous chapter, we'll notice that Haman uses none of these phrases indicating submission.

Second, her speech is *discerning*. She echoes the king's offer: "my life . . . my petition . . . my people . . . my request" (Esther 7:3). She makes clear reference to Haman's edict by using the same words: "destroyed, killed and annihilated" (v. 4; see 3:13). She identifies with her people, so that to threaten one is to threaten the other (v. 4).

Third, she is *deferential*, suggesting that only extreme circumstances have forced her to raise this issue with the king (Esther 7:4). She does not point out who the perpetrator is until the king asks (v. 5). Even then, it is only after she has described him as "an adversary and enemy" that she reveals it is "this vile Haman" (v. 6).

The way Esther approaches the king shows her wisdom about how to best present a request.

In a sense, the timing for her speech also shows her wisdom. She couldn't make her request when she first approached the king (Esther 5:3–4), because Haman wasn't there. He had to be present because otherwise he might have been able to wiggle out of the accusation. Then somehow she sensed that the timing wasn't right to answer the king at the banquet (5:5–8).

But now she has made her request She has pointed her finger at Haman. The explosion has gone off. The king leaves in a rage. And Haman is left with Esther to beg for his life (Esther 7:7).

Read Ecclesiastes
8:1–6. How does
Esther measure up
to this description
of how a wise
person acts in the
court of a king?

Jesus says we will
need to give an
account for every
careless word
we have spoken
(Matthew 12:36–37).
Reflect on how your
words have the
power to affect
others (see
Proverbs 18:21)?

Day 20

Read Esther 7:8–9

What happens next couldn't have been planned by Esther. Haman falls onto the couch where Esther is reclining. Just as his wife and wise men predicted, he literally falls. Maybe he was begging too hard. Maybe he is tipsy from too much wine. Maybe both. But he topples onto the couch just as the king walks in (Esther 7:8).

As the king was fuming outside in his garden, he must have been thinking, "What am I going to do? I authorised Haman's edict by giving him my signet ring. And he has gone and written an edict against my own wife!"

As he walks back in, a solution presents itself. He sees Haman fall "onto" his wife. Perhaps his mind flashes back to Haman asking for the royal robes and the royal horse. Perhaps he puts it all together and concludes that Haman now wants his wife! Treason! As he says, "Will he even molest the queen while she is with me in the house?" (Esther 7:8). Regardless of Haman's intentions, his action is a serious breach of royal protocol. In Persian society, a man who approached a royal concubine or wife, even accidentally, could be executed.

Straight away, the guards know what the king means (Esther 7:8). They cover Haman's face to lead him away.

Then, as it just so happens, one of the king's eunuchs, Harbona, casually slips in a morsel of choice information: "A pole reaching to a height of fifty cubits [22.5 metres] stands by Haman's house. He had it set up for Mordecai, who spoke up to help the king" (v. 9). Perhaps Harbona is implying that Haman wanted to kill someone who was loyal to the king. And so the king says, "Impale him on it!" (v. 9).

Esther couldn't have planned for Haman to build the pole. And she couldn't have planned for Harbona to add his two cents' worth. Certainly, she couldn't have planned for Haman to fall on her couch just as the king returned.

Again, the hidden hand of God is at work to accomplish His purposes. But as we can see from Esther's example, it does not mean that we just sit back and wait. We can also plan and then act, using wisdom in the opportunities that God gives us. We see too that speaking (Esther 7:9) at the right time is a sign of wisdom.

How do you feel about Haman receiving the punishment he intended for another?

The interaction between God working to accomplish His purposes and our need to act is also seen in our lives. Read Philippians 2:12–13. What do we need to do? What does God do?

Day 21

Read Esther 7:10

Today we'll see what we can learn about anger from the book of Esther. We've just seen King Xerxes' anger flare up when he sees Haman fall "onto" his wife (Esther 7:8). His fury only subsides after Haman is impaled (v. 10). Previously, the king was furious when Queen Vashti refused to answer his summons (1:12). There he responded by permanently removing her from his presence. When his anger subsides he remembered what he had done to Vashti (2:1).

The king is not the only person to burn with anger in the narrative. The two eunuchs who plotted against the king were also angry (Esther 2:21). This led to their demise (v. 23). Haman is also described as being angry. He is twice "filled with rage", both times when he saw that Mordecai refused to pay him honour (3:5; 5:9).

The king's anger leads to the removal of his queen and his chief official from his presence. Haman's anger leads to him trying to remove Mordecai from his presence. The eunuchs' anger leads them to try and remove the king, but ends with their demise. On the whole, the temper of these characters flares because they feel they have been wronged or slighted. In other words, it is a self-centred anger. They all probably had some grounds to feel wronged, but their self-centredness led to over-reaction and rashness.

The Bible warns against the foolishness of a quick temper. This warning is found in both the Old Testament (e.g. Proverbs 14:16–17, 29; Ecclesiastes 7:9) and the New Testament (e.g. James 1:19–20). "Fits of rage" are not appropriate for those who are members of the kingdom of God (Galatians 5:19–20; Colossians 3:8). Yet there are times when anger is the right response. Jesus' anger was justified; it was not the result of a personal slight. For instance, He was angry with the Pharisees, and with the moneychangers in the temple (Mark 3:5; John 2:14–16). The apostle Paul allows for Christians to be angry but our anger is to be limited, and in our anger we are to be careful to "not sin" (Ephesians 4:26–27). Let us watch ourselves, lest our anger get the better of us.

What situations cause your anger to flare?

Read Galatians 5:16–26. How can we avoid gratifying "the desires of the flesh", which include "fits of rage"?

Day 22

Read Esther 8:1–2

On the same day that Haman falls, Mordecai rises. The impaling of Haman probably provided the chance for Esther to reveal to the king that Mordecai was her relative (Esther 8:1). Haman is again described as "the enemy of the Jews" (v. 1), but now he has been executed as an enemy of the Persian Empire. As such, Haman's estate has been confiscated by the empire and given to Queen Esther (v. 1).

The king already knew Mordecai as the one who had saved his life (Esther 2:21–23; 6:1–2). Now that he also knows Mordecai's relationship to Esther, he elevates him to the equivalent of prime minister in place of Haman. So the signet ring that the king gave to Haman before (3:10) is now given to Mordecai. He now has the power to act with the authority of the king. And Queen Esther appoints Mordecai over Haman's estate (8:2). He now controls everything that Haman used to. The temporary honour that was granted to Mordecai from the king through Haman, when he was paraded around the city (6:11), is now permanent reality.

What a swift turnaround! Just the night before, Haman had built a pole for Mordecai to be impaled on. But the next day, Haman has been impaled on it instead. Now Mordecai has taken over Haman's position and possessions. At the start of the day he was destined to hang limp on a high pole; by the end of it, he is looking down from a position of power.

This turnaround is founded on the idea of justice. Mordecai saved the king's life but wasn't rewarded. He is now. By using trickery and slander, Haman schemed to destroy all of God's people but wasn't punished. He is now. Although God isn't mentioned in this turnaround, we know from elsewhere in the Bible that He is a God of justice. **As it says in Psalm 75:7, "It is God who judges: he brings one down, he exalts another."**

In God's universe, evildoers will ultimately be punished and those who do what is right will be rewarded (Ecclesiastes 12:14).

ThinkThrough

How have you experienced injustice in your life? How would you normally handle it?

Justice may not always be served in our lifetimes. Read 2 Corinthians 5:10. What assurance do we have in knowing that, one day, God will bring punish-ment and reward for every person?

Day 23

Read Esther 8:3–10

The archenemy of the Jews is dead, but the jaws of death are still open. How is Haman's edict going to be dealt with?

Again we see Esther's wisdom in the way she approaches the king with her request. She first appeals to the king by humbly falling at his feet and pleading with tears (Esther 8:3). Wisely, she does not mention the king's own role in Haman's plot. It must have been risky to approach the king uninvited for the second time, for we see that he has to extend his sceptre yet again (v. 4). Next, she asks the king to reverse the "dispatches" of Haman (v. 5). Again she starts her request with a show of submission, "If it pleases the king" (v. 5). This phrase is commonly used by those who make requests of the king (1:19; 3:9), including Esther previously (5:4). But now she also draws on her personal relationship with the king, "if he regards me with favour . . . if he is pleased with me" (8:5; cf. 7:3).

Esther's use of words is instructive. By describing Haman's edict against the Jews by using the word "dispatches" or "letters" instead of "edicts" (as used previously in Esther 1:20; 2:8; 3:14–15; 4:3, 8) she subtly suggests that they may be reversible (although they are not; see Esther 1:19; 8:8).[3] What she asks of the king is against Persian custom, and she is aware of this because she adds the phrase "if

he . . . thinks it the right thing to do" (8:5).

She then concludes her request by emphasising the effect of Haman's decree on her: "For how can I bear to see disaster fall on my people? How can I bear to see the destruction of my family?" (Esther 8:6). In other words, Esther says to the king, "If you care about me, you must do something to save my people!" In these ways, Esther's request to the king again reveals her wisdom and her courage in identifying with her people.

Also notice what she does *not* do. The official edict is unjust. But she does not rebel against the edict behind the king's back. She asks him directly. Her submissive and subtle approach ensures she does not antagonise the king by challenging his authority. **In short, she does not try to undermine the Persian system. She works within the system to achieve her goal.**

So Mordecai writes another edict to counteract Haman's edict (Esther 8:8–9). It is dispatched by express post to every corner of the Persian Empire (v. 10).

[3]See Debra Reid, *Esther: An Introduction and Commentary*, Tyndale Old Testament Commentaries (Nottingham: Inter-Varsity Press, 2008), 133.

What is your attitude towards governing authorities? Is it consistent with Romans 13:1–7?

Sometimes governing authorities will abuse their powers and we, Christians, will be persecuted (Matthew 10:16–23). How can we speak and act with wisdom in these circumstances?

Day 24

Read Esther 8:11–17

Mordecai writes an edict to counteract the first one. If you read it carefully, you'll notice that it counters Haman's edict (see Esther 3) almost word-for-word. The counter-edict allows the Jews, on the same day as the original edict, to "assemble and protect themselves; to destroy, kill and annihilate the armed men of any nationality or province who might attack them and their women and children, and to plunder the property of their enemies" (Esther 8:11).

Look carefully at the wording of the edict. Does it allow the Jews to kill whomever they like? No, the edict only allows for self-defence. The Jews could kill the armed men who attacked them. The edict could not be used as an excuse for unjustified aggression against their enemies.

When the decree went out, the Jews rejoiced (Esther 8:16). Even those from other nations declared themselves to be Jews (v. 17). Why? It's much safer to join the winning team, right? After all, not only does Mordecai write the counter-edict, he is also revealed in his full glory: "royal garments of blue and white, a large crown of gold and a purple robe of fine linen" (v. 15).

Another reason is given for the many self-declarations: "because fear of the Jews had seized them" (v. 17).

Does this remind you of anything in the Old Testament? It's similar to Rahab's response in Joshua when she sided with the Israelites against her own people. When she heard about the power of God displayed in the exodus and Israel's military victories, she said to the Israelite spies, "A great fear of you has fallen on us" and "When we heard of it, our hearts melted in fear and everyone's courage failed because of you, for the LORD your God is God in heaven above and on the earth below" (Joshua 2:9, 11).

Although the accuser of the Jews is dead, they still have to defend themselves against their enemies. Yet this little phrase, "because fear of the Jews had seized them" (Esther 8:17), tells us that God is on their side.

And once the God of heaven and earth is on your side, deliverance is a foregone conclusion.

ThinkThrough

By His death and resurrection, Jesus has defeated the great accuser (Colossians 2:13–15). Do you realise that, as Christians, our deliverance is also a foregone conclusion?

But those who don't identify themselves as Christians will not be safe from destruction. Who can you encourage to trust in Jesus as their Lord and Saviour and so be saved from eternal death?

Day 25

Read Esther 9:1–10

And so, the day arrives for the two decrees to be put into effect (Esther 9:1). The Jews gather together in all the cities to defend themselves against those who hate them. They overpower their enemies, those throughout the Persian Empire who try to harm them (v. 2). The nobles, officers, governors, and royal officials recognise Mordecai's place of power and fear him (vv. 3–4). They too help the Jews (v. 3).

With the authority given by the counter-edict, the Jews end up killing 500 men in the fortress of Susa (Esther 9:5–6), including the ten sons of Haman (vv. 7–10). All the things that Haman boasted about are now gone (see 5:11).

There is no specific mention of God in the Jews' self-defence but there are two hints that He is still working behind the scenes. First, everyone was afraid of the Jews (Esther 9:3). We discussed before how this points to people fearing not just God's people but also the power of their God (cf. 8:17). Second, and closely linked, is the phrase "no one could stand against them" (9:2). Elsewhere in the

Old Testament, this phrase points to God as the one fighting for His people and giving "all their enemies into their hands" (e.g. Joshua 21:44; 23:9). Thus, God is hidden but again we can find His fingerprints all over this episode.

How does God deliver His people from their enemies in these verses? By a reversal: "the enemies of the Jews had hoped to overpower them, but now the tables were turned and the Jews got the upper hand over those who hated them" (Esther 9:1). What happened with Haman and Mordecai is repeated on a larger scale. **God's people were on the road to annihilation, but then the opposite happens and they change places with their enemies.**

When we think about it, we are also saved by a reversal—the ultimate reversal. The king of the Jews is hung on a cross and it looks like Satan has won. But it is by His death that He defeats the great enemy and opens the way to eternal life.

ThinkThrough

Why is it that everyone, including you and I, are on the road to death and destruction (Romans 5:12)? How are we delivered from the penalty and power of sin (1 Peter 2:24)? Praise God that in Jesus, we too can enjoy a wonderful reversal.

Consider your own deliverance from Satan, sin, and death. Where in this can you identify God's fingerprints?

Day 26

Read Esther 9:11–16

In the citadel of Susa, the Jews kill 500 men, along with the sons of Haman (Esther 9:6–10). The king then asks Esther what she would like to do next (vv. 11–12). She asks for permission for the Jews to defend themselves the next day in the rest of Susa (v. 13). She also asks for the bodies of Haman's sons to be impaled and displayed as a deterrent (v. 13). By the end of the two days, another 300 men in Susa, and 75,000 in the rest of the provinces, are killed. We're horrified by this massive body count. Did the Jews go too far in defending themselves?

War and killing are never neat and tidy. Perhaps some Jews did go too far. Perhaps some Jews held grudges against their neighbours and used this chance to get back at them.

But we need to keep six things in mind:

- If Haman's plan went ahead, it is likely more people would have died. One estimate is that there were 750,000 Jews at this time.4

- The text suggests that the killing was limited to men only (Esther 9:6, 15; see 8:11).

- 75,000 may have been a small percentage of the total population of the Persian Empire.5

- Although the Jews were allowed to take the possessions of their enemies, they laid no hand on the plunder (Esther 9:10, 15–16). There is no hint that the Jews were motivated by greed.

- King Saul took the plunder but didn't kill King Agag, as he was meant to (1 Samuel 15). The Jews in Esther do the opposite: they leave the spoil, and kill the enemy, including all of King Agag's line—Haman and his ten sons. What is the narrative saying? The Jews finish what Saul should have done, in the way it should have been done.

- Relief and peace can only be experienced if the enemy is completely removed. If pockets remained of those who hated the Jews, the Jews would always be worried that they would rise up and attack them again (another reason to kill Haman's ten sons). This is similar to what we find in the oracles against the nations (see Ezekiel 28:24–26).

We can imagine how the Jews were living in fear for their lives. **Yet now they can celebrate relief from enemies and the fear of death because of their deliverance.** We are again reminded of God's hidden hand at work as we recall Mordecai's words: "relief and deliverance for the Jews will arise" (Esther 4:14).

[4] Joyce G. Baldwin, *Esther, Tyndale Old Testament Commentaries* (Leicester: InterVarsity Press, 1984), 104.

[5] The population of the Persian Empire in 500 BC is estimated to have been between 17 to 35 million people; Josef Wiesehofer, "The Achaemenid Empire" in *The Dynamics of Ancient Empires: State Power from Assyria to Byzantium*, eds. Ian Morris and Walter Scheidel (Oxford: Oxford University Press, 2009), 77.

ThinkThrough

Are we sometimes tempted to take revenge? What advice does Paul give us (Romans 12:19)?

Do you fear death? If so, why? As Christians, why is it that we can live a life free from the fear of death (Hebrews 2:14–16)?

Day 27

Read Esther 9:17–22

God's deliverance of the Jews is such an important event that it is commemorated each year. The description of the festival emphasises the reversal: from fasting, mourning, and sadness to feasting, relief, and gladness (Esther 9:22). Different days are set for the Jews in Susa (the edict had been extended one more day for them; see verse 15) and the rural Jews to celebrate (vv. 17–19). It is a time of giving presents of food to one another and gifts to the poor (vv. 19, 22). This makes sure that all members of God's community can celebrate, not just the wealthy. Sharing food brings out the social aspect of celebration and worship, and perhaps the presents remind people that the deliverance is a gift from God.[6] Mordecai records the events and establishes Purim as an annual festival. He thus makes sure that there is a yearly reminder of the deliverance of God's people (vv. 21–22).

There is a dominant note of joy in this celebration of God's deliverance. The words "happiness", "joy", or "gladness" are mentioned nine times in chapters 8 to 9 (Esther 8:16 [twice], 17 [twice]), five of which are in today's reading (Esther 9:17–19, 22). Even for Jews today, the Festival of Purim is the loudest and the most fun of all. And why wouldn't God's people be overjoyed?

This pattern of deliverance followed by rejoicing is found elsewhere in the Old Testament. For instance, Moses and the people sang a song of praise to God after He delivered them from Pharaoh and the Egyptians (Exodus 15). Deborah and Barak sang a song of praise after God delivered them from their Canaanite oppressors (Judges 5).

As Christians, we too should live a life bursting with gladness and joy! We too have been delivered. Did you notice that the Jews celebrated with joy even before their day of self-defence arrived (Esther 8:16)? Why could they celebrate? Because they knew that God was on their side. Their archenemy and accuser had been defeated. Victory was a foregone conclusion. If you think about it, we are in the same boat as the Jews before their day of self-defence. Jesus has already defeated Satan. We are saved in Jesus. Our final deliverance is a foregone conclusion.

[6] See Barry G. Webb, *Five Festal Garments: Christian Reflections on the Song of Songs, Ruth, Lamentations, Ecclesiastes, Esther*, New Studies in Biblical Theology (Leicester: Apollos, 2000), 132.

ThinkThrough

Meditate on Colossians 1:9–14. What has God delivered or rescued us from? How should we live our lives in response?

Do people more often describe you as grumpy and mournful or happy and joyful? Read 1 Peter 1:8. How can we be "filled with an inexpressible and glorious joy"?

Day 28

Read Esther 9:23–32

Today's passage continues the description of how Purim was established. An interesting aspect is how the festival got its name. Haman plotted against the Jews and cast the lot (*pur*) to find the most auspicious day to carry out his plot (Esther 9:24). Purim is the plural of *pur* (v. 26). Yet in the Old Testament, the lot is also cast to find out God's will. For instance, Joshua used lots to work out which tribes would receive which portions of land (Joshua 18:6). So the name "Purim" for the festival regularly reminds God's people of a deeper reality. Haman thought that he determined the fate of God's people by casting lots. But in reality, God's hand controlled the destiny of His people.

Esther writes an official letter to confirm the celebration of Purim (Esther 9:29–32). She uses her royal authority to add weight to Mordecai's letter. In a sense, this extra authority is needed, since this is the only religious festival in the Old Testament that is not directly instituted by God.

Esther's mention of "fasting and lamenting" (Esther 9:31) adds another feature to Mordecai's description of Purim. Mourning might seem out of place for a festival with a strong note of joy. But fasting and lamenting help the Jews to remember their situation before their deliverance (4:3, 16). It thus highlights the reversal, giving them greater reason for celebration.

Establishing regular religious festivals and seasons helps us to remember what God has done for us. After all, the problem with us is that we tend to forget. As Christians, we don't celebrate Purim. But we do celebrate Easter, which marks the ultimate reversal. In it, we commemorate the wonderful truth that Jesus "has destroyed death and has brought life and immortality to light through the gospel" (2 Timothy 1:10).

How can you make your next Easter celebration more significant? In what other ways can you remember God's goodness in your life?

Read 1 Corinthians 11:23–26. The Lord's Supper is a sacrament taken more frequently than once a year. But how is it similar in meaning to Purim? How is it different from Purim?

Day 29

Read Esther 10:1–3

As the narrative ends, we are reminded of the power and reach of the Persian Empire. Remember, this is an empire that extends across 127 provinces (Esther 1:1). It has the power to grant a suspension of taxes (2:18 ESV), and then re-impose taxes on everything under its power, all the way to the distant coastlands (on the eastern Mediterranean; Esther 10:1).

Just like at the beginning of the narrative of Esther, the Persian king's "power and might" is mentioned (Esther 10:2). He promotes Mordecai, and the Jew's greatness can be found in no less than the historical records of the kings of Media and Persia (cf. Esther 2:23; 6:1). Elsewhere in the Old Testament, the deeds of the kings of Israel and Judah are recorded in historical records (e.g. "the book of the annals of the kings of Judah", 1 Kings 14:29). Historical records are also mentioned earlier in the narrative of Esther (Esther 2:23; 6:1). The recording of Mordecai's position and actions indicate that he is an important figure. Perhaps there is even a suggestion that his status is comparable to that of the previous Israelite kings.[7]

The Persian Empire might be magnificent, but its king has shared some of that honour with Mordecai (Esther 10:3). He is only answerable to the king, just as Joseph was to Pharaoh in Egypt (Genesis 41:40). Unlike Haman, Mordecai did not seek power for his own benefit or to oppress others. Instead, he worked for the good of his people—God's people. He also spoke "peace" (*shalom*) to all his "seed" (descendants) (Esther 10:3 KJV). What this suggests is that he secured peace not just for his generation, but for future generations also. "Relief" from enemies had been won (9:16, 22); now the other side of the coin, "peace" (well-being, wholeness, and positive relationships) can also be enjoyed. Again, this rest and peace is in contrast with what Haman brought to the people (e.g. Esther 3:15).

Thank God that He uses people like Mordecai, and Joseph and Daniel before him, to work for the welfare and peace of His people, as well as for society in general.

[7] Leslie C. Allen and Timothy S. Laniak, *Ezra, Nehemiah, Esther* (Peabody: Hendrickson, 2003), 268.

ThinkThrough

In this world we will face difficulties, but how can we enjoy true peace? See John 14:27 and 2 Thessalonians 3:16.

Who in government or positions of power (cf. 1 Timothy 2:1–2) can you pray for?

Day 30

Read Genesis 12:2–3, 7

Now that we've finished reading and reflecting on the book of Esther, let's take a step back to see how it fits into the storyline of the whole Bible. In particular, we'll focus on God's crucial promises to Abraham (who was known as Abram at that time). We find these promises near the beginning of the Bible's storyline (Genesis 12:2–3, 7):

"I will make you into a great nation,
and I will bless you;
I will make your name great,
and you will be a blessing.
I will bless those who bless you,
and whoever curses you I will curse;
and all peoples on earth
will be blessed through you."
. . .

The LORD *appeared to Abram and said, "To your offspring I will give this land."*

We can summarise God's promises using an acronym: LOB. This is how they are fulfilled in the book of Esther.

Land. In the book of Esther, the Jews are outside the Promised Land, although some have returned already during the reigns of Kings Cyrus and Darius.

Offspring. Although they are outside the Promised Land, God continues to protect His people. Haman's edict threatens to wipe out the Jews across the Persian Empire, which was the whole of the known world at that time. Yet God's people must be preserved for the arrival of Jesus on earth, since He will be descended from Abraham and the Jews. So God intervenes decisively through Esther.

Blessing. By preserving and blessing the Jews, God will bless all the peoples of the world through them (Genesis 12:3). Through Jesus, a Jew, all are blessed, including us Christians today. The flipside of blessings are curses: "Whoever curses you I will curse" (v. 3). In the book of Esther, those who attack God's people are cursed by God. Part of the reason that the Jews take no spoil is because they are carrying out God's judgment.

It is important to know how the book of Esther fits into the wider storyline of the Bible. **God acts in the book of Esther so that His promises to Abraham will stand.** He is a faithful God who keeps His covenant (Deuteronomy 7:9). Praise God that all of his promises find their "Yes" in Jesus Christ!

What difference does it make to you knowing that God always keeps His promises?

Read 2 Corinthians 1:20. How does Jesus fulfil all of God's promises? What does this mean to you personally?

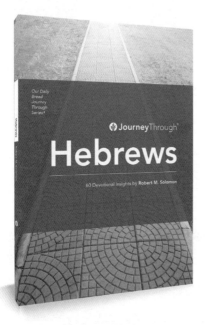

Journey Through

Hebrews

Have you ever had second thoughts about being a Christian? Sometimes it's hard to stay committed to Jesus amid the daily onslaught of worldly wisdom, tedium, and temptation. Let the book of Hebrews remind you about the Author and Perfecter of our faith; who He is, what He did, and why it matters. Be encouraged by the unique truth of a God who became a man to die in our place and who, as our eternal High Priest, will return bringing eternal rest for those who have anchored their faith in Him.

Robert M. Solomon served as Bishop of The Methodist Church in Singapore from 2000–2012. He has an active itinerant preaching and teaching ministry in Singapore and abroad. He is the author of more than 30 books, including *The Race*, *The Conscience*, *The Sermon of Jesus*, *Faithful to the End*, *Finding Rest for the Soul*, and *God in Pursuit*.

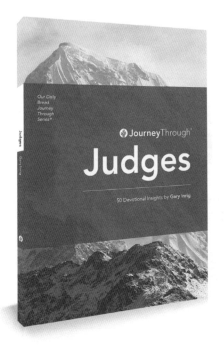

Journey Through

Judges

The book of Judges describes a low point in the history of God's people. It tells of a time of moral and spiritual anarchy, when everyone ignored God's life-giving laws and did what they thought was right in their own eyes. It is a story of disobedience and defeat. Yet the book also contains glimpses of the Israelites' capacity for greatness—when they chose to trust and depend on God. Discover God's great principles of life, and find out how we can lead powerful, productive lives in a society that is increasingly hostile to our faith.

Gary Inrig is a graduate of the University of British Columbia and Dallas Theological Seminary. An established Bible teacher and former pastor, he has authored several books, including *True North*, *The Parables*, *Forgiveness*, and *Whole Marriages in a Broken World*.

Going Deeper in Your Walk with Christ

Whether you're a new Christian or have been a Christian for a while, it's worth taking a journey through the gospels of Matthew, Mark, Luke, and John. Each gospel presents a distinct aspect of Christ and helps us gain a deeper appreciation of who Jesus is, why He came, and what it means for us.

Hear His words. Witness His works. Deepen your walk with Jesus as you follow Him through the wonderful scenes painted in the gospels.

Journey Through

Matthew

The first book of the New
Testament makes it abundantly
clear who Jesus is: the Immanuel
(God with us), and Saviour of
the world. It shows us how Jesus
fulfilled all that was predicted of
the Messiah, and how His death
and resurrection would bring
salvation and reconcile people
to God. Embark on a journey of the gospel of Matthew with
Mike Raiter, and let this truth of Jesus' eternal authority change
your walk with God. Be challenged as you take up Jesus' call
to follow Him, and discover what it means to lead a life of total
commitment to the Messiah.

Mike Raiter is a preacher, preaching trainer, and a
former Principal of the Melbourne School of Theology
in Australia. He is now the Director of Centre for
Biblical Preaching and the author of a number of books,
including *Stirrings of the Soul*, which won the 2004
Australian Christian Book of the year award.

Journey Through

Mark

Take time to go through the shortest gospel in the Bible, and you'll find it packs punch. Mark's gospel presents to us the living Christ and tells us who Jesus is, what He said, and what He did. It portrays Jesus as a man of action as well as words, and reminds us how we are to love God's people in practical, compassionate ways. Dig deeper into the book with Robert Solomon, and be amazed by what the Servant King has done for you. Follow in Jesus' footsteps, learn from His life on earth, and be led to a personal encounter with Him, so that you may become more and more like the Servant King.

Robert M. Solomon served as Bishop of The Methodist Church in Singapore from 2000–2012. He has an active itinerant preaching and teaching ministry in Singapore and abroad. He is the author of more than 30 books, including *The Race, The Conscience, The Sermon of Jesus, Faithful to the End, Finding Rest for the Soul,* and *God in Pursuit.*

Journey Through

Luke

From Mary's opening song to God her Saviour, to Jesus' last words to His disciples to preach repentance for the forgiveness of sins, the gospel of Luke is a proclamation of salvation. This salvation is for those to whom Jesus calls: the sick, the lost, the outcasts, and the broken.

How do we receive this salvation? By responding to Jesus' call: "Follow Me." But what does it mean to follow Jesus? And what will it cost us? Join the 12 disciples on their journey with Jesus and find out what discipleship really means.

Mike Raiter is a preacher, preaching trainer, and a former Principal of the Melbourne School of Theology in Australia. He is now the Director of Centre for Biblical Preaching and the author of a number of books, including *Stirrings of the Soul*, which won the 2004 Australian Christian Book of the year award.

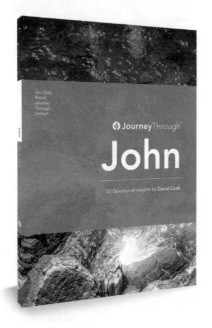

Journey Through
John

The gospel of John begins with a bold declaration: "In the beginning was the Word, and the Word was with God". It then poetically introduces Jesus Christ as God incarnate—not just God himself, but also the perfect, visible expression of an invisible God whom mankind could see, hear, touch, and relate to. Unsure of your faith? Dig into the gospel of John. Discover who this unique Son of God is and anchor your faith on solid ground.

David Cook was Principal of the Sydney Missionary and Bible College for 26 years. He is an accomplished writer and has authored Bible commentaries, books on the Minor Prophets, and several Bible study guides.

For information on our resources, visit **ourdailybread.org**. Alternatively, please contact the office nearest you from the list below, or go to **ourdailybread.org/locations** for the complete list of offices.

BELARUS
Our Daily Bread Ministries
PO Box 82, Minsk, Belarus 220107
belarus@odb.org • (375-17) 2854657; (375-29) 9168799

GERMANY
Our Daily Bread Ministries e.V.
Schulstraße 42, 79540 Lörrach
deutsch@odb.org

IRELAND
Our Daily Bread Ministries
64 Baggot Street Lower, Dublin 2, D02 XC62
ireland@odb.org • +353 (0) 1676 7315

RUSSIA
MISSION Our Daily Bread
PO Box "Our Daily Bread",
str.Vokzalnaya 2, Smolensk, Russia 214961
russia@odb.org • 8(4812)660849; +7(951)7028049

UKRAINE
Christian Mission Our Daily Bread
PO Box 533, Kiev, Ukraine 01004
ukraine@odb.org • +380964407374; +380632112446

UNITED KINGDOM (Europe Regional Office)
Our Daily Bread Ministries
PO Box 1, Millhead, Carnforth, LA5 9ES
europe@odb.org • +44 (0)15395 64149

ourdailybread.org

Sign up to *Journey Through*

We would love to support you with the *Journey Through* series! Please be aware we can only provide one copy of each future *Journey Through* book per reader (previous books from the series are available to purchase).

If you know of other people who would be interested in this series, we can send you introductory *Journey Through* booklets to pass onto them (which include details on how they can easily sign up for the books themselves).

☐ **I would like to regularly receive the *Journey Through* series**

☐ **Please send me ____ copies of the *Journey Through* introductory booklet**

Just complete and return this sign up form to us at:

Our Daily Bread Ministries, PO Box 1, Millhead, Carnforth, LA5 9ES, United Kingdom

Here at Our Daily Bread Ministries we take your privacy seriously. We will only use this personal information to manage your account, and regularly provide you with *Journey Through* series books and offers of other resources, three ministry update letters each year, and occasional additional mailings with news that's relevant to you. We will also send you ministry updates and details of Discovery House products by email if you agree to this. In order to do this we share your details with our UK-based mailing house and Our Daily Bread Ministries in the US. We do not sell or share personal information with anyone for marketing purposes.

Please do not complete and sign this form for anyone but yourself. You do not need to complete this form if you already receive regular copies of *Journey Through* from us.

Full Name (Mr/Mrs/Miss/Ms): _____

Address: _____

_____

Postcode: _____ Tel: _____

Email: _____

☐ I would like to receive email updates and details of Discovery House products.

Signature: _____

All our resources, including *Journey Through*, are available without cost. Many people, making even the smallest of donations, enable Our Daily Bread Ministries to reach others with the life-changing wisdom of the Bible. We are not funded or endowed by any group or denomination.